SPORTS HEROES AND LEGENDS

Babe Ruth

D1166458

Read all of the books in this exciting, action-packed biography series!

Hank Aaron	*Michael Jordan*
Muhammad Ali	*Sandy Koufax*
Lance Armstrong	*Michelle Kwan*
Barry Bonds	*Mickey Mantle*
Roberto Clemente	*Shaquille O'Neal*
Joe DiMaggio	*Jesse Owens*
Tim Duncan	*Jackie Robinson*
Dale Earnhardt Jr.	*Alex Rodriguez*
Lou Gehrig	*Wilma Rudolf*
Mia Hamm	*Babe Ruth*
Tony Hawk	*Ichiro Suzuki*
Derek Jeter	*Tiger Woods*

SPORTS HEROES AND LEGENDS

Babe Ruth

by Paul Mercer

BARNES
& NOBLE

NEW YORK

Another one for Laz, a Yankee fan through and through

Written by Catherine Nichols

Cover photograph: © Bettmann/CORBIS

Sports Heroes and Legends™ is a trademark of Barnes & Noble, Inc.

Barnes & Noble, Inc.
122 Fifth Avenue
New York, NY 10011

ISBN-13: 978-0-7607-3470-4
ISBN-10: 0-7607-3470-4

Printed and bound in the United States of America

10 9 8 7

Contents

America's Game

In 1939, several years after he had retired from baseball, Babe Ruth visited Honolulu, Hawaii. While on the island, he took the time to pay his respects at the grave of a man named Alexander Cartwright. Ruth had never met Cartwright. In fact, Cartwright had died three years before Ruth had been born. So why was Babe Ruth there?

Because Ruth, like all baseball players before and since, owed Alexander Cartwright a great deal. Almost one hundred years earlier, Cartwright had established the rules for the modern game of baseball, the game that would become America's favorite pastime and catapult hundreds of men, including the Bambino himself, to fame.

Cartwright, of course, didn't pull baseball out of thin air. Some version of it has been with us since our nation's earliest days. Games involving sticks and balls were brought to the colonies by the British in the 1600s. However, these games

1

were considered to be children's games, and no hardworking colonist would dare to be caught playing them. This changed by the early 1800s, as Americans had more time to devote to leisure. Rounders, a version of the English game of cricket, was very popular at this time. It was played throughout America and is considered to be the forerunner of our modern game of baseball.

Like baseball, rounders required a batter to hit a ball and run around the bases without being tagged out. Unlike baseball, though, fielders got runners out by "plugging" or hitting them with a ball. Depending on where it was played, the other rules of rounders varied a great deal.

Cartwright took some of these rules, added a few of his own, and came up with the modern game of baseball. To begin with, he specified that there should be nine players on a team. He devised the baseball diamond and stated what the distance between each base should be. Instead of hitting runners with balls for an out, fielders were required to tag runners. Cartwright also invented the position of shortstop.

Perhaps one of his most important contributions to the game was establishing foul lines. Before the foul rule was established, a ball could be hit in any direction. With foul lines, players had to sharpen their hitting skills. More importantly, foul lines created an area where spectators could safely sit and watch the game. Before then, watching baseball was more dangerous than playing it, and ball games didn't exactly draw crowds. But the foul lines changed all that—thank goodness. Just imagine what baseball would be like without its fans!

THE MYTH OF ABNER DOUBLEDAY

Alexander Cartwright wasn't always considered the father of modern baseball. In 1907 a special commission gave Abner Doubleday, a Civil War hero, that honor. The commission based its decision on a letter that claimed that Doubleday had made up the rules in 1839 in Cooperstown, New York. Later on, historians determined that this was not the case, but Doubleday's name was so lodged in the public's mind that even today some people believe that he "invented" the game.

Cartwright also helped organize the sport's first official baseball club, the New York Knickerbockers. A longtime admirer of firefighters, Cartwright named his new club after the Knickerbocker Engine Company. On June 19, 1846, the Knickerbockers traveled to the Elysian Fields in Hoboken, New Jersey, to play against the New York Nine in the first modern baseball game. Sadly for the Knickerbockers, they were trounced by a score of 23–1.

They didn't even have the satisfaction of blaming the poor results on bad umpiring. Cartwright was the umpire for the game!

Knickerbocker ball quickly became known as the New York Game. At first the game was confined to the New York–New Jersey area. Four years after Cartwright introduced the game, he caught a bad case of gold fever and headed west to find his fortune in California. On the long trip across the country he made many stops. Like a Johnny Appleseed of baseball, at each place he stayed, Cartwright taught people his new game. Cartwright eventually ended up in Honolulu, Hawaii. There he introduced baseball to the people of the island, where it became very popular.

The Civil War also helped to spread Cartwright's new sport. As Union soldiers from New York traveled throughout the South, they brought their favorite pastime with them. By the war's end it seemed like everyone was playing the New York Game, only now the name had been changed to what it is known as now—baseball.

Baseball grew more and more popular, but it was still an amateur's game. In fact, in 1857 most players agreed that no one should ever be paid for playing baseball. No paychecks meant no corruption. So when the first governing body of base-ball was formed that year—the National Association of Base Ball Players—the handful of teams involved agreed not only on rules for the game, but that no players would receive money for their time on the field. Imagine what top-dollar players like Anthony Rodriguez and Barry Bonds would say to that!

Of course, that all changed in 1869. So many teams were going against the rules and paying players off the books, the association decided to split the teams up into teams that paid and teams that didn't. This was when the first professional baseball team was formed. The Cincinnati Red Stockings traveled the country, wowing fans and winning games. In fact, they didn't lose a single game all year. Thanks to the Red Stockings' success, more professional teams formed in other cities, and in 1879 eight clubs banded together to create the National League. Today, with many more clubs under its rule, the National League still exists.

A NEW LOOK

The Red Stockings club got its name from the bright red stockings the players wore. By putting on these stockings, the team revolutionized the way baseball players dressed. Other teams took note of the snazzy knickers and long stockings and copied their design. Soon this new style of uniform had replaced the long trousers that dated back to the Knickerbockers.

In the late 1860s the unofficial Negro Leagues were also formed. Much of the country was segregated after the Civil War, and although some teams allowed black men to play on their teams, most refused. As a result teams made up of only African American players popped up all over the country. By the 1880s baseball was officially segregated, and no black player would play on a major league team until Jackie Robinson broke the color line in 1945.

In the meantime smaller leagues were being formed all over the United States, but none as big and powerful as the National League. Then in 1901, 22 years after the NL's formation, the American League was created. At first the National League refused to recognize the upstart AL. But Byron Bancroft Johnson, president of the American League, had something to say about that. He was determined to make his new league as competitive as the NL. The first thing he did was create American League teams in three cities where the National League had recently shut down squads—Washington, Baltimore, and Cleveland. It was a perfect strategy. The fans in these towns were salivating for some baseball and were ready and willing to buy tickets to see the new teams play. Then Johnson started offering higher salaries to the National League's players. Many National League stars jumped ship to play for more money in the new league, and the NL started to weaken.

Two years later the National League realized it could no longer withstand losing its players and its fans to the AL and declared the AL its equal. There was peace in baseball once again! The two leagues reached an agreement that would benefit everyone: Starting in 1903 and continuing to this day, the leagues' best teams meet at the end of each season and play each other in the World Series.

By the time the first World Series game was played, baseball pretty much resembled the game that we see played today. But that wasn't always the case. Imagine a baseball game where pitchers threw the ball underhand, the way they do in softball. The pitching distance was a mere 45 feet to home plate, not over 60 as it is today. And instead of four balls for a batter to get a walk, it took nine. One umpire was responsible for the entire field, which led to quite a few miscalls. Games took a lot longer to play and were much less exciting than they are today.

The equipment was also different. Until the 1880s fielders didn't even wear gloves. They caught the ball bare-handed. Luckily the ball was softer and mushier than it is today. However, a mushier ball meant that it didn't travel that far. Home runs were a rarity. Baseball was played as a game of strategy. Contact hitting, bunting, and base stealing were the offensive tactics most often used.

Today dozens of balls are used in a major league game. That wasn't true a hundred years ago, when only a couple of balls were used. The balls became beat up as the game went on, and if they were made uneven and therefore hard to control, the players just had to work with them. Like today, sometimes a ball was hit into the stands as a result of a home run or a foul ball. With so few balls available, ushers tried to wheedle the lucky fans who caught them into giving the balls back.

That was the game of baseball in the late 1870s. Over the next 20 years or so, the modern game as we know it was formed. In 1884 pitchers started throwing overhand. In 1889 a new rule was created declaring that if a pitcher threw four balls, the batter got a base. In 1893 the pitching distance to home plate was lengthened, and by the 1890s fielders were wearing baseball gloves similar to the ones worn today.

And so, around the turn of the century, the stage was set. Modern baseball was being played in ballparks throughout the country. Although it had been only 50 years or so since its "invention," it was already America's favorite game. Attendance was at an all-time high. New and bigger ballparks were being built to handle the crowds that had come out to see stars like Ty Cobb and Cy Young.

Meanwhile, in the bustling port city of Baltimore, a young boy was growing up. This boy, like many others in his poor neighborhood, had caught baseball fever, and he grew up playing and loving the game. Years later, when his own spectacular career was over, he would kneel in gratitude and place a flower lei on the grave of a man he had never met. It was Babe Ruth's way of thanking Cartwright for devising the game that had made it all possible.

Chapter One

The First Homer

In March 1914 a young man traveled to Fayetteville, North Carolina, by train. Although he was 19 years old, he had never ridden on a train before. He had never traveled farther than Baltimore, the city of his birth.

The young man's name was George Herman Ruth. Only a few days earlier his home had been St. Mary's, a reform school for wayward boys. There his superior ball-playing talents had attracted the notice of Jack Dunn, owner of the Orioles, a minor league team. Dunn had signed Ruth to a six-month contract and sent him to Fayetteville with the rest of the squad for spring training.

Although hitting was what Ruth was ultimately to become famous for, it was his pitching that had impressed Dunn, and it was the position of pitcher that he played in his early baseball career. Even then, though, there were signs that Ruth had another, bigger talent—that of hitting balls farther than they'd ever been hit before.

In Fayetteville the weather was terrible—nothing but rain and more rain. The team kept itself busy and dry with games of basketball, but Ruth must have been itching to get his hands around a bat. He got his chance on March 7, a Saturday, when at last the sun came out.

Without another team to play against, the Orioles were divided into two teams, the Sparrows and the Buzzards. Ruth, a Buzzard, played shortstop. As news of the game spread, a crowd of 200 or so townspeople gathered at the Fair Grounds to watch.

By the time Ruth stepped up to the plate in the second inning, the Buzzards were leading four runs to one. At his second time at bat as a professional ballplayer, Ruth not only scored, he hit a homer that sailed far into the surrounding cornfields. The crowd had never witnessed such a phenomenal hit. Years before, a ballplayer by the name of Jim Thorpe had hit what was then the longest drive in the Fair Grounds. Ruth's homer, everyone agreed, had surpassed Thorpe's by 60 feet. Not surprisingly, the Buzzards went on to win the seven-inning game with a score of 15–9.

The next day the local newspapers were buzzing with Ruth's feat. HOMER BY RUTH FEATURE OF THE GAME, *The Baltimore Sun* bragged about its hometown hero. RUTH MAKES MIGHTY CLOUT, proclaimed *The American*. The sportswriters, the fans, and Ruth's teammates couldn't have known that they had witnessed history that day. They couldn't have known that Ruth would go on to rack up a string of records, some unbroken to this day. They couldn't have known that he would become the Home Run King, the Sultan of Swat, the Bambino loved and honored by millions. On that warm spring day in March, George Herman Ruth's future was still a big question mark. But his powerful first homer gave a hint of the excitement that was to come.

Chapter Two

Wild Child

George Herman Ruth had a wild childhood. As a small boy, he roamed the streets of Baltimore, doing pretty much what he wanted. He hung out with other tough kids like himself and rarely went to school. He threw eggs and apples at passing trucks. He chewed tobacco, drank whiskey, and stole. When he was older, Ruth didn't deny his troubled past. "I was a bum when I was a kid," he said.

His parents were beside themselves. Little George, as his family called him, was his parents' first child, born on February 6, 1895. He had been a handful from the start, but now nothing they did worked. His father, George Ruth (Big George), worked long hours in his family's saloon. He didn't have time to go chasing after his rowdy son. His mother, Katherine Schamberger Ruth, was a sickly woman and also had a two-year-old daughter to tend to.

Until 1934, when he needed his birth certificate to get a passport, Babe Ruth thought his birthday was February 7, 1894. When the certificate showed that he was really a year and one day younger than he had assumed, Ruth ignored the news. He didn't subtract the year off his age, and he continued to celebrate his birthday on the seventh.

Drastic steps needed to be taken, and Little George's parents took them. On June 13, 1902, George Ruth was sent to live at St. Mary's Industrial School for Boys. There he was labeled "incorrigible," which is a fancy way of saying he couldn't be controlled. St. Mary's was a reform school, but it wasn't only that. It also took in orphans and boys whose families had fallen on hard times. There were around 800 boys enrolled when George first entered.

The school was run by Xaverian brothers, an order of the Catholic Church. From sunup to sundown the brothers made sure the boys in their charge followed a strict regime. The boys woke early every day and went to mass. After that they were kept busy with classes and workshops until late afternoon, when they had an hour or two of free time. Then it was time for supper. Lights-out was eight o'clock sharp. This routine remained unchanged throughout George's entire stay.

Because St. Mary's was an industrial school, the boys, in addition to schoolwork, learned a trade. George worked in the school's tailor shop, attaching collars onto shirts. He earned a little spending money and seemed to enjoy the work. Years later, when he was a Yankee making over $70,000 a year, he still turned the collars of his expensive shirts himself—and did a perfect job.

The first time George's parents sent him to St. Mary's, he stayed only a month, but when his parents welcomed him home, it was clear his behavior hadn't improved. George ended up back at school soon after and was in and out of St. Mary's for the next 12 years of his life. Whenever he left, his mother would miss her boy and want him home with her. When he returned, though, he would get into trouble and go back to school. After he turned 10, George pretty much stayed at St. Mary's. Although in some ways it resembled a prison with its strict rules, it still felt like home to the young boy.

One reason for this was Brother Matthias or, as the boys at St. Mary's called him, the Boss. The Boss was a formidable man. He stood six feet, six inches tall, weighed over 250 pounds, and was strong and muscular. He wasn't a man who kids could fool around with. Although he was strict, the Boss was also fair, and his young charges respected him for that.

George certainly did. He admired Brother Matthias and considered him "the greatest man I've ever known." The Boss likewise saw something in George, something that if developed might give some discipline to the wild child. That something was a talent for baseball.

---

66 *The only real game, I think, in the world is baseball.* **99**

—BABE RUTH

The favorite sport at St. Mary's was the same as America's—baseball. There were more than 40 teams at the school, organized according to age level. The best players in the school belonged to a league, which played against themselves and against other schools. George, as catcher, was the league's star player. He also played first base and sometimes took the outfield.

Although George started as a catcher, he ended up a pitcher. He credited the change in position to Brother Matthias. One day George's team was losing badly, due mainly to poor pitching. George teased the unhappy pitcher and laughed at his mistakes. The Boss headed over to him and demanded to know what was so funny. George pointed to the pitcher.

"All right, George," the Boss said. "You pitch."

George admitted that he didn't know how.

"Oh, you must know a lot about it," the Boss countered. "You know enough to know that your friend isn't any good. Go out there and show us how it's done."

George had no choice but to try. "I didn't even know how to stand on the rubber or how to throw a curve or even how to get the ball over the plate," he later confessed. Yet as he stood there on the mound, looking down at the batter, he felt like pitching was the most natural thing in the world. He had no trouble striking out batters. Before long, he was pitching for St. Mary's on a regular basis. George didn't know it as he stepped up to the mound that day, but pitching was going to catapult him out of St. Mary's and into the world of professional baseball.

❝As soon as I got out there I felt a strange relationship with the pitcher's mound. It was as if I'd been born out there. Pitching just felt like the most natural thing in the world. Striking out batters was easy.❞

—BABE RUTH

Chapter Three

The Kid Pitcher from Baltimore

The Baltimore Orioles, then a minor league team, were owned by a man named Jack Dunn. Always on the lookout for new talent, Dunn made a habit of scouting local baseball games. In 1913 an important game was going to take place between St. Mary's and St. Joseph's College, another Xaverian institution. Dunn was invited.

Both sides bragged that they had the best up-and-coming pitcher. St. Mary's had Ruth, of course, while St. Joseph's had Bill Morrisette, the star pitcher for *his* team. As the big day drew near, the students and teachers at St. Mary's grew more and more excited. Huge crowds were expected to come see the matchup between the two pitchers, including Dunn. The boys couldn't wait.

Then, one morning, it seemed like all their dreams had been dashed to smithereens. George Ruth was missing. An open window had been too much of a temptation, and he had slipped through it sometime during the night. Why did Ruth run away from St. Mary's only weeks before the big game? No one knows, but perhaps the itch to escape and seek adventure just proved too great. Whatever the reason, he was gone, and St. Mary's was desolate.

---

66 *Watch my dust.* **99**

—Babe Ruth

The school's probation officer was sent out to look for him. For three days the officer combed Baltimore's waterfront, searching for Ruth. Eventually he was found and brought back. As punishment for running away, he was made to stand alone in the school yard during recess. At the end of five days he was released, handed his mitt, and told to start practicing.

Ruth did as he was told, and by the time the big day rolled around, he was in fighting form. The boys of St. Mary's watched their dream come true. Before their astonished eyes, they witnessed Ruth striking out 22 batters for a shutout. St. Mary's dusted St. Joseph's by a score of 6–0. It was a glorious day for St. Mary's.

After the game Ruth and Dunn had a long talk about

Ruth's future as a ballplayer. Ruth must have impressed Dunn because the following February, Dunn returned to St. Mary's and signed the young pitcher to his first professional contract. The contract was for six months and the pay was $600, or $100 a month. To a poor boy like Ruth, it must have seemed a fortune.

On a Monday in early March, Ruth left Baltimore for training camp in Fayetteville, North Carolina. There had been a terrible blizzard over the weekend—the worst in 25 years—and the city was covered in snow. Ruth had to battle his way through huge drifts to meet members of his team in a hotel. From there they made it to the train station where, miraculously, their train left on schedule.

Ruth had never before been on a train, and he looked around him in amazement. Some of his new teammates took advantage of his innocence and played a joke on him. When Ruth wondered what a small hammock above his berth was for, they informed him it was for resting his pitching arm. Ruth took them at their word and that night slept with his arm slung in the hammock. He awoke the next morning with a very stiff arm. The hammock was meant to hold clothes, not arms. In Fayetteville he continued to be fascinated with trains. He'd often get up early in the morning just to go down to the station and watch the trains hurtle down the tracks.

Almost every experience was new to the wide-eyed Ruth. At the hotel in Fayetteville, Ruth became mesmerized with the elevator. He rode it whenever he could, even talking the operator into letting him run it. One day he stuck his head out the doors just as the elevator began to rise and narrowly missed losing his head.

Ruth's wonder must have amused his teammates. Most of the Orioles were much older than the 19-year-old Ruth. Five were over 30, and another was 28. Many were veterans of the game, having once played in the major leagues. Ruth, still very much a boy, must have felt out of place among these men.

Ruth got his famous nickname "Babe" while in training camp in Fayetteville. As one of the youngest players on the team and certainly the most naive, he was affectionately called Dunn's Babe. Babe was a common nickname for young ballplayers. (Around this time the Pittsburgh Pirates had a Babe Adams on their roster.) Ruth's nickname caught on with the press. Before long the name George must have seemed a distant memory to Ruth.

Despite his insecurity, Ruth was successful in training camp. He made his season debut on April 22, facing the Buffalo Bisons. Ruth was nervous on the mound, but after a shaky first inning he recovered and pitched a 6–0 shutout. He also scored two singles.

From this impressive start Ruth took off. Dunn realized he had a star on his hands and made sure Ruth knew his talents were appreciated. In May he doubled Ruth's salary to $1,200. In June he raised it again. With his first paycheck in hand, Ruth ran out and bought something he had always wanted—a bike.

❝ *That Ruth is a comer. For a kid just breaking in, he's a marvel. He's a $12,000 beauty.* **❞**
—Pat Moran, Philadelphia Phillies coach,
after seeing Babe Ruth pitch

Dunn hadn't raised Ruth's salary just to be generous. He also didn't want other teams poaching his star player. Dunn had other worries as well. The Orioles belonged to the International League. A new league had recently formed, the Federal League, and one of its teams, the Terrapins, took root in Baltimore. Excitement about the new team built, and before long Baltimore was Terrapin crazy. The Terrapins played to packed ballparks while the Orioles, who were also having a great season, watched the crowds dwindle. The low point was a game for which only 17 fans showed up.

Ruth never forgot St. Mary's and the people he had left behind. When one of the school's buildings burned and was destroyed in 1919, Ruth helped out the following year. He arranged for the school band to travel with the Yankees, his current team, in order to raise funds to repair the building.

One of the reasons Dunn had hired Ruth and other premium ballplayers was to combat the Terrapins. In one way, his plan had worked. The Orioles were now a leading ball club. By midseason the team led the league by 17 games. In spite of this success, the fans stayed away. To really rub it in, the Terrapins played in a ballpark across the street from the Orioles. Dunn watched the crowds stream past him to enter the Terrapins' stands. The Terrapins apparently knew the value of Ruth. They supposedly offered him a huge salary increase if he jumped ship and played for them. Ruth turned them down.

Dunn watched his money go down the drain and knew he

had to act. Toward the end of the season he had no choice but to sell his most outstanding players. Ruth went to the Boston Red Sox for $8,500. Although things hadn't worked out well for Dunn and his Orioles (the team sank to last place the following year), Ruth, like a cat, had landed on his feet. He was now a major leaguer!

Chapter Four

Off to Boston

Ruth joined the Red Sox in the middle of 1914. According to one teammate, "he had never been anywhere, didn't know anything about manners or how to behave." He was summed up as "just a big, overgrown green pea." His first day in Boston he won his first game as a pitcher in the big leagues, a 4–3 game against the Cleveland Indians. For his second game he was in for only three innings. After that he sat on the bench for the next four weeks before playing and winning two exhibition games.

One of the reasons Ruth warmed the bench so much was because Red Sox manager Bill Carrigan preferred to use his other new pitcher, Ernie Shore. The organization also had other plans for Ruth. The Red Sox's top minor league club, the Providence Grays, was in a race for the International League pennant. Management felt that Ruth could help the team clinch it. In mid-August he was sent down to Providence.

Ruth was understandably unhappy about the move. He had just made the majors. Going to the minors again felt like a step down. Besides, he had met a swell girl when he had come to Boston, a young waitress named Helen Woodford. He wanted to continue courting her, and that would be hard if he was stuck in Providence for the rest of the season.

❝Sometimes I still can't believe what I saw. This 19-year-old kid, crude, poorly educated, only lightly brushed by the social veneer we call civilization, gradually transformed into the idol of American youth and the symbol of baseball the world over—a man loved by more people and with an intensity of feeling that perhaps has never been equaled before or since.❞
—HARRY HOOPER, BOSTON TEAMMATE OF BABE RUTH

Once he was in Providence, though, Ruth quickly adjusted. He liked the manager, Wild Bill Donovan, who had been an outstanding pitcher in his own right, and learned a lot from him about how to throw a baseball. Donovan, likewise, was thrilled to have Ruth, a southpaw, or left-handed pitcher, on the team to complement the right-handed pitching of his current star hurler.

The fans of Providence were also happy to have Ruth. They turned out in droves, coming by automobile, by buggy, by bicycle, and by foot to witness Ruth's first game. Over 10,000 people crowded their way into the ballpark to see Ruth play.

He didn't disappoint. His pitching was a little off, but with the Grays behind in the last inning he hit a mammoth triple. The crowd went wild. The next batter up also scored, and the Grays won. Ruth continued to perform well for the rest of the season, winning nine games and helping his team capture the pennant. The Red Sox then called him back to Boston (the American League season was still going on), and Ruth pitched another winning game there. He also had his first major league hit, a double off the Yankees' Leonard Cole.

NO KNACK FOR NAMES

One of the many things Ruth was famous for was not remembering people's names. Waite Hoyt was Babe's teammate on the Yankees for 11 seasons. Still, when Waite left in 1930, Ruth said, "Good-bye, Walter." Because names gave him such difficulty, he usually stuck to calling most people Kid, which he pronounced "Keed."

The season over—a season in which he played for three teams, Baltimore, Boston, and Providence—Ruth prepared to return to his father's house. He wasn't thrilled, though, about leaving Helen behind. While in Providence he had made frequent trips back to Boston to see her. The young lovers talked it over and, even though they had known each other for only three months, decided to get married.

After a small and private ceremony, a reception was held in Baltimore. For the rest of the winter the newlyweds remained in Baltimore, living in the apartment above George Senior's saloon.

When the 1915 season started in March, Ruth kissed Helen good-bye and headed off to North Carolina for training camp. Ruth had every reason to be happy as the train chugged into the station. Only a little more than a year ago he had been living in St. Mary's without much money to his name and no prospects. He had never traveled farther than Baltimore. Now he was a married man, earning more money than his father, and with an exciting future in baseball ahead of him.

Unfortunately, that exciting world didn't take off immediately. Carrigan had plenty of ace pitchers on his team, including two spectacular lefties, so he didn't use Ruth much in his pitching rotation. Then Carl Mays, an outstanding relief pitcher, twisted his ankle and was unable to play. Carrigan put Ruth in Mays's place. His pitching impressed Carrigan, and he began to use Ruth more and more. Ruth ended the season with an exceptional record of 18 wins and only eight losses.

As a pitcher, Ruth only got up to bat every fourth day. Still, that season he managed to clobber four home runs. His fourth home run of the year even broke a window across the street from the ballpark! In these early days of baseball home runs weren't as common as they are today—the league leader in home runs in 1915 had hit seven—nor were they appreciated as much. They weren't viewed as anything special—they were just long runs. When Ruth stepped up to the plate, he made home runs exciting because he made hitting them look so easy.

Ruth hit his first major league home run at the Polo Grounds in New York when he faced off against Jack Warhop of the Yankees. Ruth's ball landed in the upper-right-field stands, and the crowds witnessing his historic event (though they didn't know it was historic at the time) were impressed with how Ruth had struck the ball. He had a powerful swing and hit the ball, according to one sportswriter, "with no apparent effort."

Like Ruth, the Red Sox were winning games the same effortless way. They ended the season with 101 wins, easily clinching the pennant. That fall they faced the Phillies in the World Series and beat them, four games to one. Ruth didn't see much action in the series since Carrigan went with his more experienced players. Still, if Ruth didn't play as much as he would have liked, he did get a huge bonus—more than double his salary—for being a winning member of a World Series team. And Ruth liked money very much.

His salary had been upped to $3,500—quite a generous amount for a rookie in those days. However, Ruth was a big spender, and he spent the money just as fast, if not faster, than he earned it. According to Carrigan, Ruth "had no idea whatsoever of money. . . . He'd buy anything and everything." To help his young pitcher, Carrigan doled out his salary to him in weekly sums.

Ruth didn't seem to resent having someone managing his financial affairs. He liked Carrigan, even if the coach did cramp his style by reining him in and insisting that he follow the club's rules. He claimed that Carrigan was the best manager he ever played for and the 1915 Red Sox were one of his favorite teams.

The following year Ruth might have had a hard time recognizing his old team. In 1916 the Federal League folded. With it went the high salaries major league teams were paying their star players to keep them from jumping ship. Ruth, who was in his last year of a three-year contract, wasn't affected, but other players saw their salaries slashed, some by as much as 60 percent.

One Red Sox player refused to return unless his salary was upped. Another, Tris Speaker, the best hitter in the club, went to training camp but wouldn't sign a contract. With a flood of players from the Federal League out of work and looking for teams to hire them, the Red Sox's owner wasn't worried. He signed a new outfielder from the Federal League and traded Speaker. The fans of Boston were outraged.

In 1916 Babe Ruth pitched 14 innings and defeated the Brooklyn Dodgers, giving him the record for the longest complete game victory in World Series history.

What had looked like a promising season now looked grim. Without their best hitter, would the Red Sox be able to repeat and bring home another championship? The answer at first seemed to be yes. The team opened strong, winning the first four games of the season. Ruth won his first four starts as well. Then the weakness in the hitting department began to show. In their first 16 games the Red Sox scored three runs or more only six times. Then the pitching began to sour.

It looked like the Red Sox were headed for a subpar season. In late June, however, things began to pick up for the team. Both their pitching and hitting improved, and they were winning games again. Ruth was spectacular, pitching 23 wins and nine shutouts. He slugged three home runs and led the league in earned run average. His best, however, was still to come.

The Red Sox clinched the pennant and were once again in the World Series, where they were matched up against the mighty Brooklyn Dodgers. The Red Sox had won the first game. Ruth was set to pitch the second. He pitched for 14 innings, the longest World Series game ever, a record that remains to this day. And what a game it was!

THE LIVELY BALL

Before 1920 baseball was played with a "dead ball." Because a hit ball didn't travel that far, home runs were much rarer than they are today. Batters didn't concentrate on hitting homers. They aimed for getting runs by bunting, place hitting, and stealing bases. Babe Ruth, of course, was the exception. He was such a powerful swinger that he clobbered homer after homer. When the team owners saw how much fans enjoyed seeing him hit them, they decided to change to a new "lively" ball. The lively ball looked just the same, but when it was hit, it flew. It turned baseball into the game we know today.

The Dodgers scored first with a home run in the first inning. In the third, Ruth hit a groundout to third base and tied the game. And that was that. For the next 11 innings the score remained tied. On both sides the pitching was excellent, with Ruth for the Red Sox and Sherry Smith for the Dodgers. Finally, at the bottom of the fourteenth inning, Boston hit the run that won the game. Throughout it all, Ruth had allowed only six hits. And from the eighth inning on, no batter got a single hit off him.

After the 2–1 win, Ruth whooped and shouted with the rest of his teammates. He hadn't pitched in the previous World Series. He was on top of the world after showing everyone what he could do if given the chance. Boston took the series, four games to one, and became world champs for the second year in a row. This time a large part of the credit went to Babe Ruth.

Chapter | Five

A Star Is Born

On April 6, 1917, five days before the start of the baseball season, President Woodrow Wilson declared war on Germany. World War I had been going on in Europe since 1914. Now the United States was involved as well. At first the war didn't have too big an effect on baseball. The season started as usual, and except for the military drills the players performed for the fans, it was business as usual. It wasn't until a year later that baseball would begin to feel restrictions from the war.

Ruth, for one, wasn't too worried about being drafted. He was a married man and therefore exempt. Besides, he had other things on his mind. Like the country, the Red Sox were undergoing big changes. Joe Lannin, the owner of the team, had just sold the Red Sox to Harry Frazee, a New York theater owner and producer. Frazee wasted no time signing his star player to a new contract.

Ruth started the new season strong and by the end of May had 10 pitching wins and only one loss. The Red Sox were in first place, although the mighty White Sox were right behind them. In spite of his strong record Ruth was often unhappy with the calls that umpires made against him and frequently complained. On June 23 he lost his temper completely. The umpire had called all three of Ruth's opening pitches balls. Ruth strongly disagreed. After each call he yelled, "Open your eyes!" When the umpire called, "Ball four!" on his last and final pitch, Ruth ran toward the plate, shouting. The two men had words, and Ruth swung at the umpire before his teammates dragged him away. Ruth, at first suspended indefinitely, was later charged with a 10-day suspension and a $100 fine.

After Ruth was reinstated, the Red Sox had a long summer

ALL BECAUSE OF RUTH!

After Ruth's ejection from the ball game on June 23, 1917, his teammate Ernie Shore replaced him on the mound. The game became an historic one as Shore took out 26 batters, not allowing them a single run or hit. It was the fourth perfect game in major league history. And it wouldn't have occurred if Ruth hadn't lost his temper!

battling the White Sox. It was a fight they ultimately lost. The Red Sox ended up in sixth place, while the powerful White Sox went on to win the World Series. As for Ruth, although his team hadn't made the pennant, he had still put together an outstanding season. He won 24 games, six of them shutouts, and had a .324 batting average, the fourth best in the league—and he wasn't even a full-time hitter.

When Ruth returned to training camp in 1918, he found that a new manager, Ed Barrow, had replaced Jack Barry, who had gone off to war. Barry wasn't the only Red Sox member to have enlisted or been drafted. There were many holes in the team and throughout the major leagues. Management hurried to plug those holes by raiding minor league teams of their best players, but many teams still had to put up with secondhand players until the war ended.

Ruth, however, was certainly no secondhand player. He was becoming a star, and with the great season he'd just had, he wanted to be paid what he was worth. But the war years were causing problems for baseball. More men off fighting translated into fewer ticket sales. Ruth wanted his salary increased to $10,000. After much bickering, he finally relented and signed for $7,000, a 40 percent salary increase.

With his contract signed, Ruth reported to camp. By the time the regular season started, he was back on the mound, his usual home. However, the Red Sox were short on good hitters, again because of the war. Barrow debated using Ruth as a hitter but decided against it. He said, "I'd be the laughingstock of baseball if I changed the best left-hander in the game into an outfielder."

By May, however, with one of his best hitters in a slump, Barrow inserted Ruth into the lineup as a first baseman who hit sixth. Ruth was still, however, expected to pitch every fourth day. And so on Monday, May 6, 1918, Ruth played for the first time in his major league career in a position other than pitcher. He responded by hitting a home run. The next day he hit another and the day after that a double. On the fourth day he returned to pitching, and while he lost on the mound, at the plate he was outstanding, hitting a single, three doubles, and a triple. His batting average was now an incredible .484!

Back in Boston, Barrow switched Ruth from first base to left field. Ruth didn't like the outfield, although it became his regular position when he wasn't pitching. Not much happened out there, and Ruth liked action. His play reflected his mood. After a 10-game batting streak, he went hitless. One sportswriter sadly proclaimed, "He didn't hit a thing, not even an umpire." Eventually, although he would have preferred to play first base, Ruth became content in the outfield.

What really mattered to him, more than anything, was hitting. After a bad cold landed Ruth in the hospital, Barrow agreed that his demanding schedule was wearing Ruth out. Ruth asked that he be permitted to give up pitching. Barrow, who had just signed a new pitcher who was doing well on the mound, agreed that for the time being Ruth could concentrate on hitting.

❝Gee, it's lonesome in the outfield. It's hard to keep awake with nothing to do.❞

—BABE RUTH

This arrangement worked just fine until Barrow lost yet another pitcher to the war. Short a pitcher and unable to get another, Barrow demanded that Ruth return to the mound. Ruth refused. He no longer considered himself a pitcher. He was an outfielder. When Barrow insisted, Ruth claimed that his pitching arm hurt and that he wasn't able to pitch. Barrow didn't believe this story for an instant.

The two men bickered throughout the month of June. Ruth insisted his arm hurt, and Barrow insisted it didn't—that he was shamming. Ruth's sore arm, however, didn't prevent him from swinging at balls. By the end of June he had hit a total of 11 home runs, an amazing number for that time, especially since the season wasn't even half over.

Barrow didn't much care about Ruth's hitting streak, at least not at the moment. His team had just slid from first place. He needed a pitcher and fast. On July 1 the situation came to a boil. Barrow chewed Ruth out after a bad play and Ruth took offense, threatening to punch his manager in the nose. Barrow quickly fined him, but Ruth had the last say in the argument. "I quit!" he shouted, and stormed out of the clubhouse.

In the first game of the 1918 World Series, Red Sox manager Ed Barrow warned Ruth to be careful when Cub outfielder Les Mann stepped up to bat, advising his starting pitcher to "dust him off a bit, for he takes a heavy toehold on the plate." Ruth promised to and was as good as his word—or so he thought. Ruth, never that sharp when it came to names and faces, hit not Mann, but another batter, Max Flack. Proud as a peacock, Ruth strutted back to the dugout. "I guess I took care of that Mann guy for you," he said. Barrow groaned. "Babe," he exclaimed, "you wouldn't know General Grant if he walked up with a bat."

Ruth might have quit the Red Sox, but he had no intention of quitting baseball. He immediately wired the manager of a shipyard team in Pennsylvania and asked to join. Because of the war many major league players had been forced to leave baseball and find profitable work. Many found jobs in factories and shipyards. Baseball teams had quickly sprung up around these workers. The shipyard was overjoyed to have a superstar like Ruth on its team and quickly said yes.

The Red Sox, of course, weren't happy. Ruth was under contract and couldn't just jump ship. A teammate was dispatched to talk to Ruth, who must have come to his senses and realized all that he was giving up. He agreed to return to the Red Sox, and he and Barrow eventually made up. Toward the end of the season he even agreed to pitch every fourth day to help the team in its race for the pennant.

---

66 *He had such a beautiful swing, he even looked good striking out.* 99

—MARK KOENIG, TEAMMATE

With Ruth back as a pitcher, the Red Sox easily won the pennant. They almost didn't get to the World Series, though. Because of the war the season was shortened, ending in early September, and the World Series was almost canceled. But at the last minute it was reinstated, allowing the Red Sox to face the Chicago Cubs.

Ruth had a magnificent series. In game one he shut out the Cubs. In game four he pitched seven scoreless innings. He now had a total of 29 scoreless innings in World Series competition. This amazing record not only broke the one set in 1905, it also lasted for 42 years. Of all of Babe Ruth's many accomplishments on the baseball diamond, it was the one of which he was most proud. The 1918 World Series ended Ruth's career as a pitcher, but what a glorious way to go out—on top.

Chapter Six

Home Run King

A fter such a fantastic year Babe Ruth was now bigger than ever. He started the 1919 season a celebrity of the top order. Everywhere he went, he was the focus of attention and very much in demand. Babe loved the crowds and the adoration. As a result he was living it up more and more. Many times when the Red Sox were on the road, Ruth stayed out until all hours of the night. Sometimes he didn't even make it back to his hotel room.

When Barrow learned that Ruth was regularly breaking curfew, he was furious. One night he sat up waiting in the hotel lobby for Ruth to return from that evening's entertainment. When Ruth had still not arrived by four, he gave up and went to bed. At the next game Ruth didn't get a hit. Barrow blamed Ruth's party boy ways for the Red Sox's subsequent loss.

Barrow was determined to catch Ruth out. He asked the

hotel's porter to let him know when Ruth returned that night, no matter how late. At six in the morning the porter knocked on Barrow's door. Ruth had just made it back. Barrow quickly rushed to Ruth's room, determined to have it out with his young star.

---

66 *Ruth made a grave mistake when he gave up pitching. Working once a week, he might have lasted a long time and become a great star.* 99
—TRIS SPEAKER IN 1921

Imagine his surprise when he found Ruth tucked into bed, the covers pulled up to his chin. Barrow immediately became suspicious. He walked over and pulled off the quilt. Ruth was dressed in his evening clothes, down to his shiny shoes. Barrow shook his head in disgust. "You're a fine citizen," he said sarcastically. Then he left, telling Ruth he'd see him in the clubhouse the following day.

At first Ruth was embarrassed over being caught. Then, as he thought about what had happened, he became angry. He didn't like being treated as if he were a naughty little boy. By the afternoon he had worked himself into a rage. When Barrow walked into the clubhouse, Ruth lashed out at him. He told his manager that if he ever checked up on him again, he'd punch him in the nose.

His teammates went silent, waiting to see how Barrow would respond. Barrow, though more than double Ruth's age, was a big man who had been a fighter in his younger days. He wasn't afraid of Ruth. He told the other players to leave and for Ruth to remain. He looked at Ruth. "I'll give you a chance to see if you can punch me in the nose."

Ruth's temper often evaporated as fast as it flared up. It did so now. Ruth dressed quickly and left the clubhouse with his fellow teammates. Barrow suspended his star player for the game. Later that day the two men agreed to a compromise. Barrow wouldn't check up on Ruth and Ruth, in return, would leave a note for Barrow telling him at what time he had gotten in. Ruth kept to the bargain, writing down the time on pieces of paper before slipping them under Barrow's door. Whether the

---

BABE RUTH'S BAT

Who invented the modern baseball bat? None other than Babe Ruth. He was the first player to order a bat with a knob at the end of the handle. In 1926 Louisville Slugger produced the bat with which he hit 29 home runs.

times he scribbled were the actual times he got in, though, was anybody's guess.

Although Ruth had troubles off the field, on the field was a different matter. Ruth once again had a spectacular season. He still occasionally pitched a game as a favor to Barrow, but he was primarily a left fielder. Now that he hit every day, instead of every fourth day as a pitcher, his batting statistics soared sky-high.

Unfortunately, the Red Sox as a team didn't do nearly as well. They started the season a strong favorite to repeat as World Series champions for yet another year. After a promising start, though, the pitching staff hit a slump that it didn't recover from. By May it was obvious that the Red Sox were out of the pennant race. They ended the season in a disappointing sixth place.

As Barrow became aware that the Red Sox weren't in contention, he used Ruth more and more to draw in the crowds. That season Ruth broke home run records right and left. On July 29 he hit his sixteenth home run, tying the American League record set in 1902 by Ralph Seybold. A little more than two weeks later he hit home run number 17, breaking the record. There was still more than two months to go in the season. What more could Ruth do?

The major league record of most home runs was 24, set by Gavvy Cravath in 1915. Fans held their breath as Ruth continued to hit home runs. Would this record also be broken? During Labor Day weekend he drove in number 24. Babe Ruth was now bigger than the pennant race. Wherever he played, the crowds came out to cheer him on.

Ruth's twentieth home run of 1919 was his fourth grand slam of the year. No player had ever before hit four base-filled home runs in one season. It remained an American League record for 40 years.

One record remained to be broken. Baseball researchers discovered that in 1884 a player by the name of Edward Williamson had hit 27 home runs for the Chicago Colts. The circumstances, though, were a bit unusual. In 1883 Williamson had had only two home runs. In 1885 he had three. How, then, had he managed 27 in 1884? The answer was obvious, once you knew where to look. In 1884 the Colts had played in a different ballpark, where right field was only 215 feet from home plate.

Although most of Williamson's home runs were probably not strictly legitimate, the record still stood. It was up to Ruth to knock it down. He did so in dramatic fashion in New York's Polo Grounds. Not only was it the longest hit ever recorded at the

Polo Grounds, it also tied the score for the Red Sox, who until then were losing one–zip.

But Ruth wasn't through. He hit number 29, his final home run of the season, in Washington during the last weekend of the regular season. This final home run gave Ruth another record. With it he had hit at least one home run in every city of the league, a feat no other baseball player had accomplished. Babe Ruth was now, without a doubt, baseball's home run king.

Red Sox owner Harry Frazee should have been enjoying his star hitter's success and the hefty income it brought in at the gate. Unfortunately, Frazee was plagued by money troubles. As a Broadway producer, he was losing money on his shows. As a baseball owner, he was deeply in debt. To solve his financial woes, Frazee had no choice but to sell some of his best players. Still, he hung on to Ruth.

By the end of the season, though, he had no choice. After his fantastic season Ruth would justifiably want a huge salary increase. Frazee couldn't afford it. Also, a big loan he owed was

After being sold to the Yankees, Ruth scored more home runs than the entire Boston Red Sox did in 10 of the next 12 seasons.

being called in. He needed money and fast. On January 5, 1920, the newspapers announced that Frazee had sold Babe Ruth, Boston's pride and joy, to the New York Yankees for $100,000 and a big loan.

If only Frazee had had a crystal ball. Although the deal was profitable, in the long run it was disastrous. Babe Ruth turned the mediocre Yankees into world champions, while the Red Sox sank to the bottom of the standings. Boston fans must have sensed that the end had come. They were furious with Frazee for selling their beloved Ruth. One fan summed it up thus, "I figure the Red Sox is ruined."

As for Ruth, he assured his new manager, Miller Huggins, he would play as hard for his new team as he had for his old. Coming off a 29 home run season, that was some promise.

The Curse of the Bambino

When the Red Sox sold Babe Ruth to the Yankees, they had won five World Series, the most by any club at that time. After the sale the Red Sox appeared in only four World Series, losing each one in game seven. Some Boston fans feel that this string of bad luck is more than just a coincidence. They say it is "The Curse of the Bambino."

Chapter Seven

Ruth Conquers New York

Ruth hit New York like a tornado. He loved the city's bright lights and its unending nightlife. The fans, in return, adored him. His popularity soared, and everywhere he went, fans besieged him. The city's Italian immigrants honored him with a new nickname, the Bambino, Italian for "babe."

The Bambino got off to a slow start at the plate, however. He didn't hit his first homer until May 1, 1920. In typical Ruthian style, when he did finally connect, he hit big. The ball zoomed high over the Polo Grounds roof.

After that, Ruth took off. By midseason he had passed his 1919 record of 29 home runs. The Yankees organization was thrilled with its new ballplayer. Until recently the Yankees had been a second-tier ball club. Now, with Ruth, they were in the race for the pennant.

In the end the Yankees had to be satisfied with a third-place finish. Still, they couldn't have been too disappointed. Because of Ruth, attendance at the Polo Grounds had skyrocketed. With over one million fans filling the stands all season, the Yankees set a new major league record in attendance.

66I swing big, with everything I've got. I hit big or I miss big. I like to live as big as I can.99

—Babe Ruth

Ruth's hitting packed them in again and again. He continued to set records all season. On July 30 he hit home run number 30, breaking his own record of 29 set the year before. He ended the season with a total of 54 home runs in all. To put this achievement in context, that year only one other team in the league hit more than 44 home runs—that's with all their players' homers *combined.*

His other achievements were also awe inspiring. He batted .376, scored 158 runs, batted in 137, and stole 14 bases. Many baseball experts consider Ruth's first season as a New York Yankee to be the single-best season any major league hitter has ever had.

Then again, a mighty fine case could be argued for his next season as well. He surpassed his home run record of the previous year, hitting 59 this time. He also led the league in runs batted in, runs scored, total bases, and walks.

He and his teammates amassed 98 wins, and for the first time in their team's history the New York Yankees nailed the American League pennant and were in the World Series. They faced another New York team, the Giants. The two teams even shared the same ballpark, the Polo Grounds, so the entire series was played in New York.

The Giants and the Yankees played very different types of baseball. The Giants, a conservative team, favored the by now old-fashioned approach to baseball. They focused on pitching to win games. The Yankees, on the other hand, were a power-hitting team and they had baseball's leading power hitter, Babe Ruth.

Unfortunately for the Yankees, Ruth injured his elbow and had to sit out the last two games. The Yankees lost both. Still, in the games he was in, he slammed 15 homers. They weren't enough, however, and the Yankees lost the series.

The Yankees' familiar pinstripe uniform was created for Babe Ruth. The vertical stripes were added so that he would look thinner.

To make some extra money, Ruth had signed up to go on a barnstorming tour after the World Series was over. These postseason exhibition tours were popular in the days before television. It gave people in small towns a chance to see famous players they wouldn't ordinarily see. Ruth enjoyed hamming it up before the crowds and, even more, he enjoyed the $25,000 paycheck he'd receive.

There was a problem, though. While the baseball establishment allowed regular exhibition games, it frowned on its World Series stars going on the tours, fearing it would devalue ticket sales. The new baseball commissioner was determined to enforce the law prohibiting World Series players from barnstorming. Ruth knew he was breaking the rules by signing on, but as in many things, rules didn't matter much to him.

And so, at the end of the baseball season, he packed his bags and went to play for The Babe Ruth All Stars. Kenesaw Mountain Landis, the new commissioner, was furious. He thought Ruth was directly challenging his authority and demanded that he return. Ruth's reaction was, "Aw, tell the old guy to go jump in a lake." However, the tour didn't do well, and when one of the Yankee owners pointed out that he was hurting the Yankees as well as himself, Ruth agreed to wrap it up.

Although Ruth had cut the tour short, Landis believed he needed to show Ruth who was boss. He fined him $3,362—his

George Ruth Jr. at age 18 (center) in his team picture from St. Mary's

Taking a swing in his early days with the Boston Red Sox

Warming up his pitching arm

Two legends: Babe Ruth and Lou Gehrig

The Babe steals home.

Shaking hands with his former teacher from St. Mary's, Father Benjamin, during the 1927 World Series

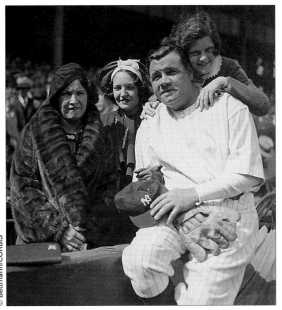

The Ruth family on opening day at Yankee Stadium, April 24, 1934

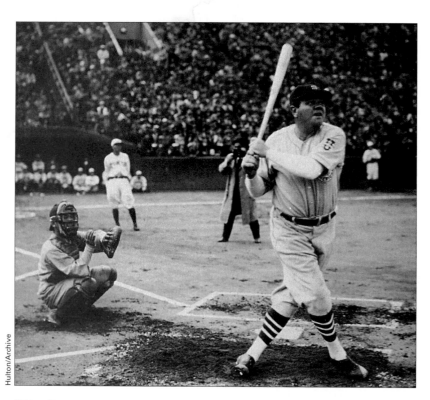

"Tokyo Babe" hits a home run at Miji Shrine Stadium in Tokyo, Japan, in 1934.

Signing autographs for a swarm of adoring fans in 1944

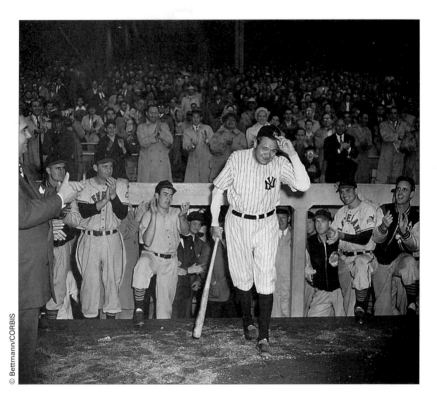

The Babe makes his last appearance at Yankee Stadium for the facility's silver anniversary celebration on June 13, 1948.

share from the World Series winnings—and suspended him for the first six weeks of the season. The lost money didn't bother Ruth, but not playing did. He went to Landis and begged him to let him join the team sooner. Landis not only refused, he lectured Ruth on his failure to respect authority.

Up to this point in his career Ruth's fortunes had been steadily rising. Each year he improved, breaking his own incredible records. He must have felt that he could do no wrong and that the fans would always be behind him. His career was like a rocket, zooming to the stars. But in 1922 Babe Ruth crashed.

STRIKEOUT AT THE PLATE

The year 1922 was an off-season for Ruth. Perhaps nothing shows this better than his face-offs against a young pitcher named Hub Pruett. Pruett, a southpaw for the St. Louis Browns, was a less than impressive pitcher with a 29–48 record. Still, in 1922 he managed to strike Ruth out 13 times in Ruth's first 21 trips to the plate. Years later Pruett, who had become a doctor, visited Ruth and thanked him for putting him through med school. "If it wasn't for you," he told Ruth, "no one would have heard of me."

After his suspension was lifted, Ruth was back with the team, but he wasn't the same player he had been the year before. For one thing, he was out of shape. For another, he still hadn't managed to control his temper. His fights with umpires continued, and he was suspended five more times that year. Once he even lunged into the stands after a heckler who called him a bum for throwing dust on an umpire.

Every strike brings me closer to the next home run.
—BABE RUTH

Although he knocked in 35 home runs that season, he batted a dismal .118. The fans were disappointed in Ruth, and they let it show. For the first time in his career he was regularly booed. It didn't help matters that the Yankees had increased his salary to $52,000 at the start of the season. In the 1920s that was an awfully large amount of money. Home Run Baker, another top hitter of the time, was only making $16,000. Sportswriters and fans felt if Ruth was making so much money, he should deliver.

Babe Ruth's poor performance continued in the World Series after the Yankees won their third-straight pennant. After 17 times at bat Ruth had only one single and one double to show for it. The Giants swept the series, four–zip.

After the disappointing series Ruth attended a dinner party at the Elks Club in Manhattan. Also at the party was a rising young politician by the name of Jimmy Walker, who would later become mayor of New York City. Walker scolded Ruth for his bad behavior and poor performance that year. He reminded him of the debt he owed to New Yorkers, especially the children who adored him. He ended his speech by asking, "Are you going to keep on letting those little kids down?"

Ruth had a soft spot for children, and Walker's remarks hit home. Ruth promised to change his ways. He intended to work out in the off-season and get into top shape again. He promised to work hard in the coming season.

THE HOUSE THAT RUTH BUILT

On April 18, 1923, the Yankees opened a new stadium. Called "the House That Ruth Built" because of all the money Ruth brought in through ticket sales, Yankee Stadium was a big improvement over the old Polo Grounds, which the Yankees had shared with the New York Giants. Ruth wowed the 75,000 fans who had come to see him by hitting the stadium's first home run. "Kids will be hitting them when I'm gone," he said, "but I'm kind of glad I hit the first one."

Ruth proved to be a man of his word. He trained all winter and reported to camp fit and ready to play. And what a season he had! He led the league with 41 home runs, batted a career-high .393, had 205 hits, and stole 17 bases. Because of the fear he inspired in pitchers, he was walked 170 times.

By working hard and staying out of trouble, Ruth led his team to their first World Series championship. Unlike his performance the previous year, Ruth's effort was superb in the 1923 series. He hit three home runs and scored eight runs in six games. For his efforts that year he was named the league's Most Valuable Player.

Babe Ruth was back on top.

Chapter Eight

In Hot Water

Ruth managed to stay out of trouble in 1924. He had another great season, and although the Yankees didn't make the pennant, finishing second to the Washington Senators, Ruth compiled an impressive record. Besides swatting 46 homers, he led the league with a .378 batting average.

By the next year, though, Ruth was once again in hot water. He had gradually given in to bad habits and was once again eating and drinking too much as well as keeping late hours. He began the 1925 season seriously overweight, having ballooned to over 250 pounds.

Not only did he report to spring training camp out of shape, he had also caught a bad case of the flu. At first he was just barely able to practice with the team, but by the time exhibition games rolled around, Ruth was again hitting homers. His health didn't hold out for long, though. His fever returned, and he

A Ruthian Diet

Ruth's appetite was enormous. His teammates were constantly amazed at the amount of food he could put away. Henry Hooper recalled, "He'd order half a dozen hot dogs, as many bottles of soda pop, and stuff them in one after the other. That would hold him for a couple of hours, and then he'd be at it again."

began having stomach pains. Ruth, ever the trouper, continued to play. Then one day, while on a train platform, he collapsed.

After being examined by a doctor, Ruth was diagnosed with an intestinal attack and sent back to New York to recover. On the train he collapsed again, this time hitting his head on a washbasin. By the time the train pulled into Penn Station, Ruth was delirious and passing in and out of consciousness. He was rushed by ambulance to Saint Vincent's Hospital, where doctors discovered he had an intestinal abscess. Surgery was scheduled. The operation was a complete success, although it did leave Ruth with a scar several inches long.

As all this was going on, a rumor popped up that Babe Ruth had died. In London, where Ruth was extremely popular, a newspaper even announced his death. Afterward Ruth's illness was dubbed "the bellyache heard round the world."

Ruth was out of commission for over six weeks. He rejoined his team at the end of May. Yankee management wanted Ruth to recuperate longer, even for the rest of the season if that was what he needed. But Ruth was adamant. The team needed him, and he needed baseball. Playing baseball was as necessary to him as air and water.

❝ *I was a babe and a boob.* **❞**

—BABE RUTH, 1925

Ruth returned, but he wasn't his old self. He was batting a mere .250 and hitting very few home runs. Still weak from his ordeal, he looked terrible. He was 30 years old now, no longer a young athlete. Many sportswriters and others connected with baseball suggested that Ruth's best years were over.

The Yankees' manager, Miller Huggins, might have agreed with that assessment. Huggins had tried countless times to rein in the team's leading hitter. Ruth, however, was openly contemptuous of Huggins, calling the tiny, five-foot-seven manager "the Flea."

Huggins was powerless to control Ruth when Ruth was batting up into the stratosphere. As long as Ruth was hitting, he was off-limits. But by the summer of 1925 Ruth wasn't playing well, although he was still living the fast life. Time after time he broke the curfews Huggins set.

Huggins decided he had to let Ruth know who was boss. He called the club's owner, Colonel Jacob Ruppert, and sought his approval for what he was about to do. Ruppert backed Huggins 100 percent.

---

66 *Confidentially—and you can print this—Miller Huggins is dumb.* **99**

—BABE RUTH, 1925

The next time Ruth sauntered in late to the clubhouse, Huggins stopped him in his tracks. "Don't bother getting dressed, Babe," he told the slugger. "You're not playing today." Huggins also informed his star player that he was fining him a whopping $5,000.

Ruth was outraged. As he saw it, he had just come to the clubhouse a little bit late. Why was Huggins overreacting? Ruth had a temper, and he let it show now. He yelled and cursed at Huggins, but Huggins, even though he was six inches shorter and a hundred pounds lighter, didn't back down. He told Ruth that before he put on a Yankee uniform again, he was going to have to "apologize for what you said, and apologize plenty."

Ruth, his temper still blazing, spoke to the press. He declared that Huggins was incompetent and that he was the reason the Yankees were having such a bad season. The press delighted in the story and egged Ruth on. Ruth said that either Huggins had to go or he wouldn't return next year as a Yankee. He went to see Colonel Ruppert, fully expecting the club's owner to overrule Huggins and reinstate him.

Ruth was in for a nasty surprise. Ruppert made it clear that he supported Huggins. He told Ruth that he had gone too far. It was up to Ruth to apologize and make amends with his manager.

66*I admire a man who can win over a lot of tough opponents, but I admire even more a man who can win over himself.*99

—YANKEES' MANAGER MILLER HUGGINS,
TALKING ABOUT BABE RUTH

Ruth returned to New York with his tail between his legs. He went to the clubhouse to see Huggins, but Huggins refused to talk to him. The Yankees were once again winning, and Huggins was in no hurry. He wanted to make sure that Ruth got his message.

For nine agonizing days Huggins kept Ruth waiting. Then he called Ruth into his office, and the two men talked. Huggins insisted that Ruth apologize to him in front of the entire team. A humbled Ruth did. The following day he hit his 300th home run.

Ruth was back. Again. And although he continued to over-indulge his love of food and drink and nightlife, he was never again seriously out of shape. And he never again challenged Huggins. Ruth had learned his lesson.

 In 1924 Columbia University proved what many people had long suspected. They ran a few tests on the Babe and determined that he had extraordinary physical powers. In the tests he was given, Ruth scored higher than 90 percent in coordination. His hearing and eyesight were superior to those of five out of six people. He also possessed nerves of steel. Only one person in 500 had better "nervous stability."

Chapter Nine

The Greatest Player on the Greatest Team

Ruth spent the winter seriously working out at a gym. When he arrived at training camp, he weighed 212 pounds and was in the best shape he'd been in for years. His hard work paid off. Ruth had an outstanding season. He scored 47 home runs and led the leagues in walks, runs scored, and hitting percentage. He missed only a few games.

With Ruth back to his old self, the Yankees rebounded. The year before, they had finished in seventh place. In the 1926 season they jumped right back to number one, winning the pennant by three games, and were the favorites to win the World Series over the St. Louis Cardinals.

The Cardinals surprised everyone, however, by winning two of the first three games. Ruth hadn't performed well in these games, hitting only two singles at his 10 at bats. He more than made up for this in game four, when he slammed his first pitch.

Home run number one. In the third inning he swatted home run number two. Then in the sixth inning he walloped a ball out of the ballpark, the longest home run ever hit in St. Louis. It brought Ruth's total to three. No baseball player had ever hit three homers in a World Series game. Once again Ruth had made history.

---

66 *If I'd tried for them dinky singles I could've batted around six hundred.* **99**

—BABE RUTH

The Yankees won games four and five, but the Cardinals tied up the series in game six. The next game would decide which team would wear baseball's top crown. As usual, Ruth figured greatly in the outcome, although not in the way he had hoped. The game came down to the ninth inning, with the Cardinals leading 2–1. Their pitcher, Grover Cleveland Alexander, already had two outs by the time Ruth came up to bat for the last time. Alexander, no doubt fearing the mighty Babe, walked him. The next batter up was Bob Meusel. Before he had a chance to swing his bat, though, Ruth tried to steal second. He was immediately thrown out and the game was over. The Cardinals were World Series champions, all thanks to Babe Ruth.

Ed Barrow, the Yankees' general manager, told Ruth it was the only dumb play he'd seen him make. Ruth shrugged off the criticism. He had gambled and lost. Ruth wasn't one to cry over spilled milk. Besides, there was always next season.

And what a season that was! The 1927 Yankees are still considered by many baseball fans to be the best team ever. A look at the statistics backs up the claim. They won an amazing 110 games, putting them 19 games ahead of the Philadelphia Athletics, the second-place team. The Yankees also led both leagues in team batting average, earned runs, and home runs. A good portion of the team's home run record, of course, was due to one Babe Ruth, who amassed an impressive 60 of them, breaking his own 1921 record.

Perhaps one reason for Ruth's many homers was the fact that Lou Gehrig had recently joined the Yankee lineup. A spectacular hitter in his own right, Gehrig began challenging Ruth for the title of home run champ that year. With 38 home runs by August, Gehrig was three ahead of Ruth.

In 1927 Ruth hit 14 percent of all the home runs in his league. For a baseball player to do that today, he'd have to hit over 300 home runs.

Ruth, always competitive, responded to the challenge. He kept slugging them out and soon left Gehrig in the dust. Would he, however, be able to break his old record of 59? With four games left in the regular season, he hit number 57, a grand slam. Three games remained. He hit numbers 58 and 59 in the following game. One more to go with two games remaining. Ruth didn't keep his fans in suspense. On September 30, in the next to last game, he swatted in number 60. As homers go, it wasn't an especially spectacular one. It went down the right field line and just narrowly missed being called a foul.

The Promise

Babe Ruth always had a soft spot in his heart for children. During the 1926 World Series he promised a hospitalized young boy that he would hit a home run for him. The boy, 11-year-old Johnny Sylvester, had been injured in a fall from a horse. Ruth kept his promise and how. He belted not one, but three homers! Afterward he paid a special visit to Johnny in the hospital.

Still, a home run is a home run, and this one was historic. According to one newspaper's account, as the crowds cheered, "the Babe made his triumphant, almost regal tour of the paths.

He jogged around slowly, touched each base firmly and carefully and when he imbedded his spikes into the rubber dish . . . hats were tossed liberally and the spirit of celebration permeated the place."

This spirit of celebration continued when the Yankees swept the Pittsburgh Pirates in the World Series. Against the mighty Yankees, the Pirates really didn't stand a chance. During a practice session, before any game had been played, the Pirates sat in the grandstands and watched the Yankees slam ball after ball over the fence. Wilbert Robinson, manager of the Brooklyn Dodgers, declared that the Pirates were "beaten already."

Although the 1928 Yankees weren't as strong a team, they still managed to clinch the pennant. They faced their old nemesis the St. Louis Cardinals in the World Series. Unlike the 1926 series, though, this time the Yankees won, sweeping the Cardinals in four games. Ruth once more put on quite a show. In 16 times at bat he had 10 hits, making his batting average an

---

❝ The way a team plays as a whole determines its success. You may have the greatest bunch of individual stars in the world, but if they don't play together, the club won't be worth a dime. ❞

—BABE RUTH

astounding .625. It was the highest ever in a World Series game. Three of those hits were home runs, and once again, all three were hit in the same game.

The homers were hit in the last game, the only one in which the Cardinals put up a fight. In the seventh inning they led the Yankees by a score of 2–1. Ruth, who had hit the one run in the game, a homer, came up to bat and missed two strikes by Willie Sherdel, the Cardinals' pitcher. Ruth then momentarily turned his head to talk to the catcher. Sherdel quickly pitched his third ball without a windup. In the regular season such "quick pitches" were legal and Ruth would have been out. However, baseball management had decided to declare these pitches illegal during World Series games. The umpire ruled in favor of the Yankees. Sherdel would have to do the pitch over.

The Cardinals were outraged. They argued the call, but in the end they had no choice. With the Cardinal fans booing him, Ruth stepped up to the plate and let fly home run number two, tying the score. As he jogged around the bases, he waved to the crowd, even as most of them jeered.

Ruth's third and final home run came in the eighth inning. Then he capped his superb day on the field in the ninth inning, making a one-handed catch of a foul fly for the last out. The Yankees ended up winning the game and the championship.

Home Run Heroes

Ruth's record of most home runs in a season lasted for 34 years. Then in 1961 Roger Maris, another Yankee, hit 61. Maris, however, hit his home runs while playing in a 162-game season. Ruth hit his in a season that had eight fewer games. In 1998 the Cardinals' Mark McGwire shattered Maris's record with 70 home runs. A mere three years later the Giants' Barry Bonds swatted an amazing 73 home runs in 2001. Will Bonds's record stand? Only time will tell.

No team had ever before swept two World Series in a row. The Yankees had proven themselves to be one of the great teams of all time. And they owed much of that title to one man: Babe Ruth.

Chapter Ten

The Called Shot:
Was It or Wasn't It?

The year 1929 started on a sad note for Babe Ruth. On January 11 his wife, Helen, died in a house fire that had been started by poor electrical wiring. At the time of her death Ruth and Helen had been separated for three years. Ruth, however, still had fond feelings for Helen and their times together. He was shattered when he learned of her death.

Six years earlier Babe and Helen had adopted a little girl, Dorothy. Dorothy was away at school at the time of the accident. A few months later, when Ruth married his longtime girlfriend, Claire Hodgson, he brought Dorothy to live with them. Claire also had a daughter, and in a novel move Babe adopted Julia, Claire's daughter, and Claire adopted Dorothy.

While Ruth's home life was undergoing changes, so was life with the Yankees. For two years the Yankees had been the undisputed stars of the American League. Now the Philadelphia

Athletics took over. For the next three years they dominated baseball. The Yankees, on the other hand, started the 1929 season strong but soon fell into a slump. They finished in second place, 18 games behind the Athletics.

By September, Ruth had already had a distressing year, but it was to get even worse. Miller Huggins, the manager Ruth had sparred with and grown to respect, became extremely ill. On September 20 he went into the hospital. Five days later he was dead.

Ruth took his manager's death hard. The team heard the news in the middle of a ball game in Boston. Afterward, in the clubhouse, Ruth openly wept. He told a newspaper reporter, "It's one of those things you can't talk much about. You know what I thought of Miller Huggins, and you know what I owe to him." At the funeral Ruth was one of Huggins's pallbearers.

With Huggins's death, the Yankees had to look for a new manager. Ruth wanted the job. He felt that with 16 years of experience in baseball under his belt and having played in so many positions, he more than qualified. In those days there were many player-managers, so his request wasn't that unusual.

Ruth, however, wasn't seriously considered for the position. As Barrow once told him, "You can't manage yourself, how do you expect to manage others?" Instead Bob Shawkey, a former pitcher, was made manager.

Ruth accepted the decision, but he wasn't happy about it. Ruth liked to feel appreciated, and so, when his contract expired, he demanded a hefty increase. At first he asked for $100,000. Ruppert counteroffered with a $5,000 raise, which would up Ruth's salary to $75,000, not a bad piece of change by any means. Ruth turned it down. For the first time in his career he became a serious holdout.

Ruth went to Florida to practice with the team. As opening day neared and he still had no contract, he became nervous. He loved baseball so much that he couldn't imagine the season starting without him. On opening day he signed a new contract, one that guaranteed him $80,000 for two years. At the time the president of the United States, Herbert Hoover, earned $75,000. When someone pointed out to Ruth that he was making $5,000 more than the president, he responded, "Why not? I had a better year than he did."

He had a better year in 1930, too. He hit 49 home runs—three of them in one game. He had done this twice in World Series games but never in the regular season. The Yankees, unfortunately, didn't do so well. Under Shawkey they floundered, ending the season in third place. Shawkey was fired, and the search for a new replacement began.

Ruth once again petitioned for the job. This time he was sure the Yankees would consider him. They didn't. They hired

Joe McCarthy, ex-manager of the Chicago Cubs. McCarthy was the kind of manager who demanded discipline. Under his reign he instituted new rules. Players had to wear jackets and ties when not in uniform. There was to be no more card playing in the clubhouse.

Ruth resented McCarthy, and he wasn't shy about saying so. He felt that he deserved to be manager. McCarthy was no fool. He knew how Ruth felt, and he wisely didn't push the Babe. While he held the other players accountable for their actions, he let Ruth slide. Once when a rookie player and Ruth both came late to the clubhouse, McCarthy looked straight past Ruth and bawled out the rookie for his tardiness.

With their strong new manager the Yankees improved immediately. They ended the 1931 season second behind the Athletics. Ruth also had a superb season. He led the league in hitting most of the time, ending with a .373 average. Together he and teammate Lou Gehrig led the league in home runs. Both had 46.

The next year Ruth once again had a great season. His batting average was .341, and he had 137 runs batted in. He also walloped 41 homers, although it was the first year since 1925 that he didn't lead the league in home runs.

The Yankees were also superb. With McCarthy as their manager the team made their way back to the top. By season's end they had won 107 games, taking the pennant easily. In the World Series they came up against the Chicago Cubs.

Like in many World Series games, a lot of bench jockeying, or taunting, went on between the two top teams. The 1932 World Series had more than its share, and as always, Babe Ruth was in the thick of it.

❝ *Why don't you read the papers? It's all right there in the papers.* **❞**

—BABE RUTH, RESPONDING TO
WHETHER OR NOT HE HAD CALLED HIS HOME RUN

In the first two games, held in Yankee Stadium, Ruth led the Yankees as they taunted the Cubs, calling them cheapskates. A former teammate of the Yankees, Mark Koenig, had recently joined the Cubs and had helped the club dramatically. Yet when it came time to decide how to divide up the World Series money, Koenig had only been voted a measly half share.

Throughout the first two games Ruth continually teased the Cubs about how cheap they were. In turn the Cubs insulted Ruth, saying he was old and fat and past his prime. He couldn't have been too much past his prime, though, since the Yankees trounced the Cubs in both games.

Game three was played in Chicago's Wrigley Field. The Chicago fans had heard about the ribbing their team had taken in New York, and they were waiting for the Yankees—especially for Ruth. In the ballpark almost 50,000 fans greeted the Yankees by booing them. When Ruth appeared on the field, lemons were thrown at him. Ruth was in a good mood, so he threw them right back.

The game didn't begin well for the Cubs. In the first inning Ruth hit a three-run homer off the starting pitcher, Charlie Root, putting the Yankees in the lead 3–0. By the fifth inning, however, the Cubs had rallied and the game was tied at 4–4. Then Ruth came up to bat.

THE BABE RUTH STORY

In 1948 a movie about Babe Ruth's life, *The Babe Ruth Story*, was filmed. The movie showed Babe Ruth, played by William Bendix, calling the shot. The film company wanted Charlie Root, the pitcher of that fabled game, to portray himself. Root turned them down flat, saying, "Not if you're going to have him pointing."

Boos filled the ballpark. Another lemon bounced onto the field. The Cubs' bench taunted Ruth as he faced Root. The first pitch was a strike. The crowd cheered. Ruth, in response, held up one finger. The next two pitches were balls. Root pitched again. Another strike! The crowd was on its feet. One more strike and the mighty Ruth would be out.

Ruth held up two fingers and was heard to say, "It only takes one to hit it." The Cubs continued to taunt him. What happened next has been disputed to this day. Some say that Ruth gestured to the bleacher over center field, implying he would hit a home run there. Others say he was gesturing to the pitcher, Charlie Root, or to the Cubs' bench.

❝ *He pointed like a duelist out where he was going to hit the next one, and hit it there.* ❞

—PAUL GALLICO, *NEW YORK DAILY NEWS* SPORTSWRITER

Where he gestured is almost beside the point because what happened next was so remarkable in itself. Root let go his pitch and Ruth swung with all his might. He hit a home run over center field, the longest that had ever been hit at Wrigley Field. The Cubs' bench was silenced. As he ran around the bases, he raised his clasped hands over his head in victory.

And victory it was! The Yankees went on to win the game and the next as well, sweeping the Cubs in four games. Ruth was overjoyed. He said, "That's the first time I ever got the players and the fans going at the same time. I never had so much fun in all my life."

---

66 *I'm not going to say he didn't do it. Maybe I didn't see it. Maybe I was looking the other way. Anyway, I'm not going to say he didn't do it.* 99

—JOE MCCARTHY, YANKEE MANAGER

The question remains: Did he or didn't he call the shot? After weighing the evidence, most sport authorities today seem to agree that Ruth was pointing to the Cubs' bench, not signaling to the bleachers. Ruth himself gave different accounts of the day. In his autobiography he claimed that he did call it. During an interview, though, he said, "I didn't exactly point to any spot. All I wanted to do was give that thing a ride out of the park."

In the end, it doesn't matter. By giving that ball a ride out of the park, Ruth put the Cubs firmly in their place and showed them that he was still king of the home run.

ANOTHER CALLED SHOT?

A teammate of Ruth's, Waite Hoyt, claimed that Ruth called a home run in Boston once. A fan there was needling Ruth, and the comments finally got to him. He looked straight at the fan and then pointed to the seats above right field. A home run followed. After rounding home plate he stopped, faced the fan, and bowed.

Chapter Eleven

An All-Star for All Times

At the start of the 1933 season there was no denying that the mighty Babe's powers were fading. With the Great Depression at its worst, Ruth was forced to take another cut in salary. He was now paid $52,000 a year, the amount he was paid in the 1920s. In spite of the pay slash he was still, amazingly enough, the highest-paid player in baseball.

On the field he was slow and plodding. Often other players had to step in and finish games for him. While he had a respectable 34 home runs that year, he was no longer the premier hitter he once was. Jimmie Foxx of the Philadelphia Athletics had eclipsed him. His slowing down also affected the Yankees; the team finished second to the Washington Senators.

Ruth wasn't ready to throw in the towel, though. In the first ever All-Star game, played in Chicago's Comiskey Park, Ruth showed he still had what it takes. In the third inning he let fly a homer, the first ever in an All-Star game. Later, in the eighth inning, he fielded a long fly ball. The American League won the game, 4–3.

Ruth also demonstrated he could still pitch as well as hit. In the last game of the season Ruth took to the mound for one last time to commemorate his 20 years in the major leagues. He faced the team he had started with, the Boston Red Sox. Ruth gave it all he had and beat his former team by a score of 6–5. Afterward his arm was so stiff that when the fans applauded him, Ruth tipped his cap with his right hand, unable to lift his left.

With the season finished, Ruth looked ahead to the following year. He had often claimed that he would retire after his twentieth season, but he decided he still had at least another year in him. He hadn't given up on his dream of managing the Yankees. The Yanks, however, were just as determined not to hire him.

Another team, however, was interested in Ruth as a player-manager. Frank Navin, the owner of the Detroit Tigers, believed that Ruth's popularity would boost his team's sagging ticket sales. He asked Ruth to come to Detroit to discuss the matter and work out a deal. Ruth, who was all set to go on a trip to Hawaii, felt that Navin and his offer would wait until he got back. Navin, however, feeling slighted, signed another manager, ending Ruth's only real chance to manage a major league team.

The 1934 season was Ruth's final season as a New York Yankee. It wasn't a good one. The aging slugger batted a mere .288 and hit 22 home runs. For the second year in a row the Yankees didn't win the pennant, finishing the season seven games out of first place.

When the season was over, Ruth and some fellow major leaguers traveled to Japan to play baseball. In Tokyo all the players, but especially Ruth, were given a warm welcome. The ballparks were sold out, and before long Beibu Rusu became a household name in Japan.

Ruth didn't disappoint his new fans. In 17 games he batted .408 and scored 13 home runs. He also amused them. Once when it was drizzling, Ruth fielded first base holding a parasol over his head.

While Ruth was swatting balls in Japan, back in New York deals concerning him were being made. The Yankees were looking to get rid of Ruth gracefully. Clearly past his prime, the big slugger had earned $45,000 the previous year. Knowing how much Ruth wanted to manage, the Boston Braves approached the Yankees. Emil Fuchs, the club's owner, was ready to offer Ruth the opportunity to play for the Braves and to be the team's assistant manager with the understanding that if things worked out, he would eventually become manager.

MOST HOME RUNS RECORD

Babe Ruth's record of most home runs stood for almost 40 years. In 1974 another Boston Brave, Hank Aaron, broke the record. Over time Aaron hit 755 home runs, 41 more than Ruth, a record that still stands today. However, in all fairness to the Babe, it should be noted that Aaron required about 4,000 more times at bat to do so.

Fuchs, whose team was losing money, knew that Ruth would be a surefire draw on the field, especially playing in Boston, the city where his professional career had begun. Ruppert, the Yankees' owner, who had claimed he would never let Ruth go to another team, changed his mind. A satisfactory plan was worked out between the two clubs. All that remained was for Ruth to agree.

❝ *All ballplayers should quit when it starts to feel as if all the baselines run uphill.* **❞**

—BABE RUTH

Ruth returned from his trip in early February. Although he was interested in going to the Braves, he still tried one last time to become manager of the Yankees. Ruppert gently told him that he was satisfied with McCarthy, the current manager, and that Ruth should seriously consider the Braves' offer.

He did and, after 15 seasons, hung up his Yankee uniform and put on the Braves'. Unfortunately for both sides, the experiment wasn't a successful one. While Ruth had an exceptional opening day, hitting a two-run homer and diving to catch a fly ball, his game quickly deteriorated. The Braves lost many games and before long had sunk to last place.

If Ruth disappointed the Braves, then just as surely the Braves disappointed Ruth. Fuchs's promise to Ruth about becoming a manager was an empty one. He never had any intention of Ruth managing, and when Ruth discovered this, he felt like a fool. The two men quarreled, and Ruth, realizing his time as a player had finally come to an end, asked to be placed on the retired list.

RUTH THE ACTOR

Next to Babe Ruth, the next-best hitter on the Yankees was Lou Gehrig. In 1939 Gehrig was diagnosed with a nerve disease that, two years later, he was to die from. When Hollywood made a movie about Gehrig's life, called *The Pride of the Yankees*, Babe Ruth was cast to play himself. By all accounts, he was a natural actor. In one scene he got into his part so much that he hurt his hand when he punched it through a window.

Fuchs, though, convinced Ruth to continue. An important road trip out west had been set up. Many of the cities they were visiting had planned Babe Ruth Days in his honor. Ruth reluctantly agreed to keep playing.

It was during this road trip, while playing the Pittsburgh Pirates, that Ruth made his final stab at greatness. In the first inning he hit a two-run homer. In the third he hit yet another. In the fifth he hit a single that drove in a run. And in the eighth, with the bases empty, Ruth swung with all his might and hit his third amazing homer of the game.

The pitcher, Guy Bush, declared he had never seen a ball hit so hard before or since. Ruth might have been "fat and old, but he still had that great swing. Even when he missed, you could hear the bat go swish."

The home run was the longest one ever hit in Pittsburgh's Forbes Field. The usher who went to find out where it landed was told it had hit a roof and bounced into a lot. There a boy picked it up and scampered off with it. That boy probably had no idea of the value of his find. For that ball was Ruth's 714th home run, the last one of his long career in baseball.

The Legend Lives On

Not long after his 714th home run, Babe Ruth retired. Except for part of one season in 1938 when he accepted a coaching job with the Brooklyn Dodgers, he was out of professional baseball for good. But he didn't want to be. He continued to hope that a managing position would open up. None did. Instead the Babe spent his days playing golf, which was, next to baseball, one of his great passions.

As the years passed, Ruth remained in the public eye, still a much loved figure. When he was spotted in the Yankee box, he would get more cheers than any of the current players. Still, as much as he enjoyed watching the games, he missed playing. In 1936 baseball showed its appreciation by electing him into baseball's Hall of Fame. He was one of the first five players ever elected.

A few years after this great honor, Ruth suffered two mild heart attacks. Later he developed pneumonia and had to be hospitalized. Ruth recovered from these setbacks, but in 1946 he experienced pain over his left eye. He thought the pain was due to a sinus headache, but when he went to have it checked out, it turned out to be something much more serious.

Doctors discovered a cancerous tumor in the side of his neck. They were able to remove most but not all of it. Ruth was never told he had cancer, though by the end of his life he probably suspected the truth. He told one visitor that "the termites" had got him.

To show their appreciation for their ailing star, the Yankees declared April 27, 1947, Babe Ruth Day. All the major league teams held celebrations, but the biggest and grandest was the one in Yankee Stadium, the house that Ruth had built. Almost 60,000 fans crowded the ballpark to see their hero. It was a much different Ruth who faced them. Because of his illness he had lost a great deal of weight. As he spoke into the microphone, his voice came out in a horse croak, again a result of the illness, which affected his larynx.

He hadn't prepared a speech. Instead he spoke from the heart. He spoke about his great love of baseball.

"You know," he said, "this baseball game of ours comes up from the youth. That means the boys. And after you've been a boy, and grow up to know how to play ball, then you come to the boys you see representing themselves today in our national pastime. The only real game in the world, I think, is baseball. As a rule, some people think if you give them a football or a baseball or something like that, naturally, they're athletes right away. But you can't do that in baseball. You've got to start from way down, at the bottom, when you're six or seven years old. You can't wait until you're fifteen or sixteen. You've got to let it grow up with you, and if you're successful and you try hard enough, you're bound to come out on top, just like these boys have come to the top now."

In his speech Ruth might have been talking about himself. For who else personified baseball more? He had first played the game as a small boy growing up in the hard streets of Baltimore. Later, at St. Mary's, it was baseball that saved him. It launched him on his career and provided him with more than a means of making a living. It gave him joy. For Babe Ruth, maybe more than any baseball player before or since, loved the game with all his heart. And just as much as he loved baseball, baseball loved him right back.

Babe Ruth died on August 16, 1948. But his legend never will.

PERSONAL STATISTICS

Name:

George Herman Ruth

Nicknames:

Babe, Sultan of Swat, Bambino

Born:

February 6, 1895

Died:

August 16, 1948

Height:

6' 2"

Weight:

200–245 lbs.

Batted:

Left

Threw:

Left

BATTING STATISTICS

Year	Team	Avg	G	AB	Runs	Hits	2B	3B	HR	RBI	SB
1914	BRS	.200	5	10	1	2	1	0	0	0	0
1915	BRS	.315	42	92	16	29	10	1	4	21	0
1916	BRS	.272	67	136	18	37	5	3	3	16	0
1917	BRS	.325	52	123	14	40	6	3	2	12	0
1918	BRS	.300	95	317	50	95	26	11	11	66	6
1919	BRS	.322	130	432	103	139	34	12	29	114	7
1920	NYY	.376	142	458	158	172	36	9	54	137	14
1921	NYY	.378	152	540	177	204	44	16	59	171	17
1922	NYY	.315	110	406	94	128	24	8	35	99	2
1923	NYY	.393	152	522	151	205	45	13	41	131	17
1924	NYY	.378	153	529	143	200	39	7	46	121	9
1925	NYY	.290	98	359	61	104	12	2	25	66	2
1926	NYY	.372	152	495	139	184	30	5	47	145	11
1927	NYY	.356	151	540	158	192	29	8	60	164	7
1928	NYY	.323	154	536	163	173	29	8	54	142	4
1929	NYY	.345	135	499	121	172	26	6	46	154	5
1930	NYY	.359	145	518	150	186	28	9	49	153	10
1931	NYY	.373	145	534	149	199	31	3	46	163	5
1932	NYY	.341	133	457	120	156	13	5	41	137	2
1933	NYY	.301	137	459	97	138	21	3	34	103	4
1934	NYY	.288	125	365	78	105	17	4	22	84	1
1935	BB	.181	28	72	13	13	0	0	6	12	0
Totals		.342	2,503	8,399	2,174	2,873	506	136	714	2,211	123
World Series (10 years)											
		.326	41	129	37	42	5	2	15	33	4

Key: AVG: batting average, **G:** games, **AB:** at bats, **2B:** doubles, **3B:** triples, **HR:** home runs, **RBI:** runs batted in, **SB:** stolen bases

PITCHING STATISTICS

Year	Team	W	L	PCT	ERA	G	GS	CG	IP	H	BB	SO	SHO
1914	BRS	2	1	.667	3.91	4	3	1	23	21	7	3	0
1915	BRS	18	8	.692	2.44	32	28	16	217.2	166	85	112	1
1916	BRS	23	12	.657	1.75	44	41	23	323.2	230	118	170	9
1917	BRS	24	13	.649	2.01	41	38	35	326.1	244	108	128	6
1918	BRS	13	7	.650	2.22	20	19	18	166.1	125	49	40	1
1919	BRS	9	5	.643	2.97	17	15	12	133.1	148	58	30	0
1920	NYY	1	0	1.000	4.50	1	1	0	4	3	2	0	0
1921	NYY	2	0	1.000	9.00	2	1	0	9	14	9	2	0
1930	NYY	1	0	1.000	3.00	1	1	1	9	11	2	3	0
1933	NYY	1	0	1.000	5.00	1	1	1	9	12	3	0	0
Totals		94	46	.671	2.28	163	148	107	1219.7	974	441	488	17

World Series (2 years)													
		3	0	1.000	0.87	3	3	2	31	19	10	8	1

Key: W: wins, **L:** losses, **PCT:** percentage, **ERA:** earned run average, **G:** games, **GS:** games started, **CG:** complete games, **IP:** innings pitched, **H:** hits, **BB:** bases on balls/walks, **SO:** strikeouts, **SHO:** shutouts

BIBLIOGRAPHY

Berke, Art. *Babe Ruth.* New York: Franklin Watts, 1988.

Creamer, Robert W. *Babe: The Legend Comes to Life.* New York: Simon & Schuster, 1974.

Macht, Norman L. *Babe Ruth.* New York: Chelsea House Publishers, 1991.

Ritter, Lawrence S. *The Story of Baseball.* New York: William Morrow & Company, 1999.

Smelser, Marshall. *The Life That Ruth Built.* Lincoln: University of Nebraska Press, 1975.

WEB SITES

www.baberuth.com

The official site has a photo album of the great one.

www.baseball-almanac.com/players/p_bruth0.shtml

Lists all 60 of Ruth's 1927 home runs; includes the date for each one and the pitcher he faced.

www.thebaseballpage.com/past/pp/ruthbabe/

Tons of info about the Babe.

www.historychannel.com/speeches/archive/speech_268.html

Listen to Ruth's moving farewell speech to baseball.

INDEX